You Think You Know Giraffes

Trace Taylor

You can tell a male from a female because the hair on the horns of the male is worn off from fighting other males.

Giraffes have **horns**.

Giraffes talk to other giraffes using infrasonic signals that people can't hear.

Giraffes have **ears**.

Giraffes have excellent eyesight. They can spot predators from far away. When they see danger approaching, they alert the other animals to the threat.

Giraffes have **eyes**.

Giraffes have special muscles they use to open and close their nostrils.

Giraffes have **noses**.

Giraffes' favorite food is the leaves of the acacia tree. Acacias have vicious thorns, but the giraffes don't care because their lips and tongues are extra tough.

Giraffes have **mouths**.

Giraffes have four stomachs, just like cows. They chew and rechew the 75 pounds of leaves and twigs they eat every day.

Giraffes have **teeth**.

Giraffe tongues are 2 feet long and are used like a car's windshield wiper to clean gunk and bugs out of their eyes.

Giraffes have **tongues**.

Males use their long necks to fight with other males. The giraffe with the longest neck usually wins.

Giraffes have **necks**.

8

The patterns and colors of giraffe hair help the giraffes blend into their environment. Color and pattern vary due to where the giraffes live and what they eat.

Giraffes have **manes**.

The front legs of giraffes are longer than their back legs. They can run very fast, but get tired quickly.

Giraffes have **legs**.

10

Giraffe hooves are the size of dinner plates. When defending their babies, giraffes can kill lions with a kick from their front legs.

Giraffes have **hooves**.

Giraffes have the longest tail of all mammals. Their tails can grow up to 8 feet long.

Giraffes have **tails**.

Coaching Tips for Parents and Teachers

Kids love to read READLINGS to parents and teachers because they CAN. Try these helpful tips.

Adults

- Read the book title and the first few pages to your child.

- Model using your finger to keep track of where you are.

- When your child can't figure out the picture, have him/her use the first letter sound as a clue.

- Remember that reading is problem solving. Help your child use all available clues.

Ready-to-Read Child

- Uses the patterns and pictures to read the rest of the book.

- Points to each word as he/she reads it.

- Uses the first letter sound to help with tricky pictures.

- Has FUN!

Can you match the words to the pictures?

tongue

mouth

legs

horns

necks

Giraffe Words

acacia thorns

giraffe eating thorny acacia tree

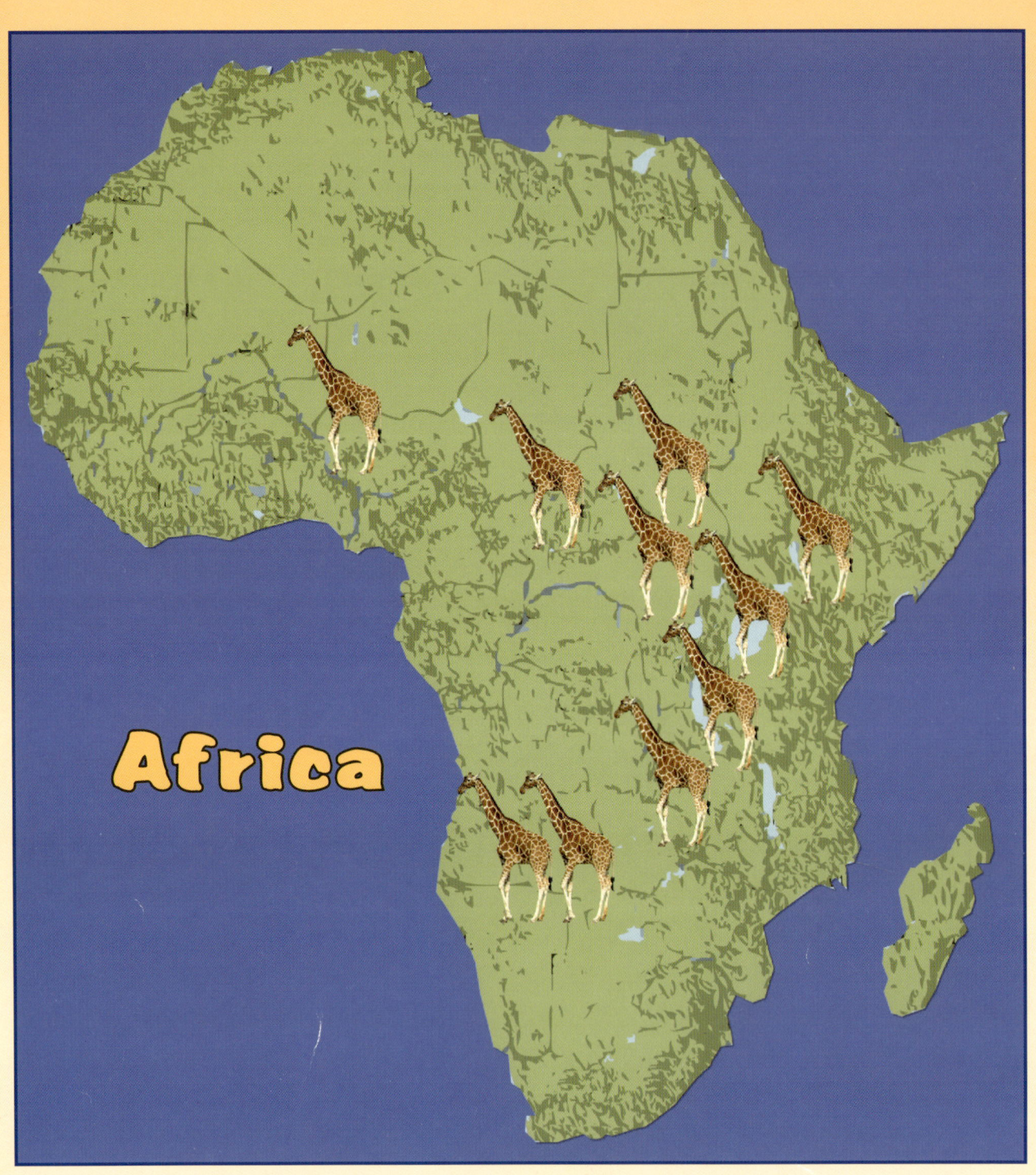

Who lives with the giraffe?

Rhinos can weigh as much as a pick-up truck. They love to eat sweet, low growing grasses and grains. These big lawn mowers often share water holes with the giraffe.

Rhino

Baboons live in huge groups called troops. These big troops can be very loud when they sense danger. Their loud calls of alarm warn the giraffe and other nearby animals of danger.

Baboon

When this small but powerful cat catches food, it likes to hide the food in trees. Sometimes even giraffes end up on this cat's dinner plate.

Leopard

The cape buffalo can weigh as much as 10 refrigerators. Huge herds share the plains and savannas with the giraffe. This is good for giraffes because even hungry lions avoid these buffalo.

Cape Buffalo

When lions go hunting, the giraffe had better look out because these big cats like the taste of baby giraffe.

African Lion

Red-billed oxpeckers spend the day riding around on the giraffe and other animals. They pick off and eat ticks that might otherwise infest the animals and drive them crazy.

Oxpecker